Cary Grant

A LIFE IN PICTURES

Cary Grant

A LIFE IN PICTURES

JENNY CURTIS

MetroBooks

MetroBooks

An Imprint of Friedman/Fairfax Publishers

Library of Congress Cataloging-in-Publication Data

Curtis, Jenny,
        Cary Grant: a life in pictures   /   by Jenny Curtis.
                    p.   cm.
        Filmography: p.
        Includes bibliographical references and index.
        ISBN 1-56799-565-9
        1. Grant, Cary, 1904   —Portraits. 1.Title.
PN2287.G675C87   1997
791.43'028'092—dc21   97-24188

Editor: Francine Hornberger
Art Director: Jeff Batzli
Designer: Garrett Schuh
Photography Editor: Karen Barr

Color separations by Ocean Graphic International Company Ltd.
Printed in China by Leefung Asco Printers Ltd.

10 9 8 7 6 5 4 3 2 1

For bulk purchases and special sales, please contact:
Friedman/Fairfax Publishers
Attention: Sales Department
15 West 26th Street
New York, NY 10010
212/685-6610   FAX 212/685-1307

Visit our website:
http://www.metrobooks.com

To Mom and Dad, whose classy taste
in movies made this possible

Acknowledgments

Thanks to Zoë Dimandopoulos, Gael McSweeny,
and the rest of the E-mail Warbrides for their help
and encouragement; The Muni Theater in St. Louis for their
use of materials; and Tim McGreevy. Thanks also to
Francine Hornberger and Karen Barr for their
help and patience.

CONTENTS

Introduction

Archie Leach

A bove: An advertisement for the Pender Troupe, where Archie Leach (Cary Grant) got his start in acting. The Penders not only became a foster family to him, but the traveling vaudevillians also taught him the discipline and professionalism that became his trademark throughout his entire career.

O pposite: Archie Leach in 1910. Archie's mother, Elsie, babied him, keeping the future actor in dresses (as was the custom in Edwardian England) and short pants longer than was the norm.

eft: Douglas Fairbanks and Mary Pickford on their honeymoon. Archie had a life-changing moment when he met these famous honeymooners in 1920 on the HMS *Olympia*. At the time, the Penders were on their way to an extended two-year engagement in New York. Archie was impressed by Fairbanks' suntan, and he vowed he would himself get plenty of sun. Eventually he used his perpetual tan as a substitute for theatrical makeup, and that fine, tawny look helped preserve his film career into the 1960s.

There is a scene in *None but the Lonely Heart* (1944) in which Cary Grant sips champagne with a mobster in a nightclub. "What is this stuff?" he asks innocently, and the mobster laughs. The audience laughs, too, because the idea of Grant not recognizing the taste of champagne is absurd. One supposes that he was weaned on it, and that even as a teenager he must have worn a tuxedo. The Cary Grant persona is such a creature of the world of nightclubs, champagne, heiresses, and big band music that it is difficult to imagine that he came from a much darker place.

Cary Grant was born Archibald Alec Leach, the son of a pants presser, in Bristol, England, on January 18, 1904. His mother, Elsie, was a class-conscious Victorian, and his father, Elias, was a handsome man with a dragoon's mustache. Elias enjoyed vaudeville and had a reputation as a bit of a stage-door Johnny. Elias and Elsie's first son died before Archie was born and their marriage was already greatly troubled when Archie came into the family. The Leaches weren't exactly impoverished, but neither were they well off. And, if you were born into the working class in 1904 England, chances were good you'd die there.

In 1912, Elias left the family for a year for a higher-paying job in nearby Southampton, where he had an affair and a son with a woman named Mabel Bass. But Elias returned home when he discovered he couldn't afford two households. When Archie was ten, he came home from school to find his mother missing. It was years later that he learned she had been committed to the Fishponds Sanitarium. Biographers differ on whether Elias committed Elsie because she was truly ill or because it was an easy way to end his marriage. Years later, after Grant had achieved stardom, he rescued his mother from the institution.

Archie found a way out of Bristol when visiting the Bristol Hippodrome as a boy. In 1917, he got a job backstage while Bob Pender and his Troupe of Comedians were playing. Pender's teenage pantomime performers and stilt walkers were always looking for replacements for the boys who'd gone off to World War I. Archie wrote a false letter of introduction, supposedly from his father, in order to get into the troupe, and at thirteen he ran away from home to join them. It didn't take his father long to catch up with him. Archie returned to school until he was nearly sixteen (the legal leaving age) and then got expelled. His father willingly

Right: Archie Leach did a season of summer stock at the Muny Theater in 1930 in St. Louis, Missouri, where he posed for this publicity photo. As you can see from his hesitant smile and rumpled pants, he hadn't yet perfected the suave, urbane image he would present as Cary Grant. Around this time he took a screen test at the East Coast division of Paramount. He was rejected for having sloped shoulders and bowlegs, but later that year he became a contract regular in the Schubert Musical Theater, earning a steady $450 a week. As the rest of the country was settling into the Great Depression, Archie was tooling around New York in his Packard Phaeton wearing a coonskin coat. With his dark good looks and English manners, he was a popular escort for debutantes. At this time, he was able to finagle a second screen test at the West Coast division of Paramount. Paramount put him in a short musical feature, *Singapore Sue*, and signed him to a three-year exclusive contract.

took him back to Bob Pender. As luck would have it, a few years after his first glimpse into this world, he was headed to America with a first-rate vaudeville act. Archie Leach would not return to England until 1933, when he was a movie star and could safely say he'd come a long way.

He was not an overnight success by any means; after a decade of small parts and frequent firings, he managed to make his way into Hollywood. His new name, Cary Grant (the first part taken from a character in a play he'd been in and the second picked at random from a list), seemed to suit the tall, dark, and handsome man he'd become. Archie Leach had been the name of a bow-legged, slope-shouldered vaudevillian who was always trying a bit too hard to seem happy. This new fellow had a refined elegance and a mysterious way that the camera seemed to adore. Cary Grant was suave, sophisticated, urbane.

Cary Grant's image was carefully and painstakingly constructed, pieced together from bits of Douglas Fairbanks, Rex Harrison, Ronald Coleman, and with an air of mystery provided by the dark past of Archie Leach. It was this new persona, Cary Grant, that captivated the world for thirty-six years in seventy-four films.

Chapter One

Cary Grant

Above: Archie Leach changed his name to Cary Grant for his first full-length feature film, *This Is the Night* (1932). He was billed below nearly all of his costars, including Lily Dimita, pictured here. Grant was relegated to the sidelines for most of the pictures he made in his first two years under contract with Paramount. Few people have actually seen much of his early work. Fifteen of his first twenty films are currently out of print.

Opposite: In *She Done Him Wrong*, Grant's naivete quickly crumbled as his character, Captain Cummings, capitalized on Lady Lou's (Mae West) rebellious sexuality. Even though he was clearly out of his depth when Lou made her advances, there was always a hint of the urbane sophisticate on his face. Grant credited West with helping his comic delivery, and the influence West's natural comic timing had on Grant's performance style is apparent in his later films.

Above: Cary Grant and Tallulah Bankhead in *The Devil and the Deep* (1932), also starring Gary Cooper and Charles Laughton. Grant's main function in this movie, and at Paramount in general, was that of a second-string Gary Cooper. In addition to taking small parts in Cooper's films, Grant filled in when the bigger star was unavailable.

Below: Grant and screen goddess Marlene Dietrich in *Blonde Venus* (1932). The film was Grant's first as leading man playing opposite a big star. Though the film was directed by Eric Von Stroheim, *Blonde Venus* was not well received by either critics or audiences. Grant was "acting with his hands in his pockets," as he later described his early career. He showed little flair in the under-written gangster role of Nick Townsend, but he did seem to be in his element in nightclub scenes like this one.

Above: Grant with Randolph Scott in a publicity photo from the early 1930s. Grant and his fellow Hollywood actors thrived during the worst of the Great Depression. In order to make their stars seem like average working folks, Paramount arranged a series of photographs of Grant and his housemate, Scott, in a variety of homey poses. This series of pictures had the unintended effect of fueling rumors about the nature of Grant's and Scott's relationship.

Above: Cary Grant and Randolph Scott celebrated their birthdays together on the Paramount lot in January 1933. The two actors were born less than a week apart, so actress Nancy Carroll presented the pair with a joint birthday cake.

Opposite: An early beefcake photo of Cary Grant on the Paramount lot. The most hotly debated issue among Grant's numerous biographers is the contention that he was bisexual. The inclusion of Grant in the books *Queers in History* and *The Celluloid Closet* has won him a new audience in the gay community, while some of his fans, along with academic biographer Graham McCann, have doggedly tried to preserve Grant's reputation as a heterosexual. Whatever the answer, it is clear that Grant's image is still potent in people's imaginations. And it is likely that Grant, who always tried to brush the question off as ridiculous, would find the current debate undignified and silly.

Above: If Grant seemed awkward as the aggressor in *Blonde Venus*, he was right at home being hit on by Mae West in *She Done Him Wrong* (1933). The story that West spotted Grant on the Paramount lot and said, "If he can talk, I'll take him," has become part of Hollywood mythology, but studio records show Grant's name came up in reference to the part from the beginning.

Right: Grant with actor Richard Arlen on the Paramount lot. Arlen appeared with Cary in the studio's all-star version of *Alice in Wonderland* (1933). While Arlen played the Cheshire Cat, Grant was stuck, miserably, behind a heavy mask as the Mock Turtle.

Above: Cary Grant and Mae West in *I'm No Angel* (1933), the story of a female lion tamer who falls for a straitlaced business-man. Critics were quick to point out that the movie lacked the breezy sexuality that made *She Done Him Wrong* so enjoyable, but that didn't keep audiences away. *I'm No Angel* was one of Paramount's biggest hits that year.

Below: Cary Grant with his new bride, Virginia Cherrill, in Rome on their honeymoon. The two were married at Caxton Hall, Westminster, on February 9, 1934. But their wedding trip was marred as his mother, still in Fishponds Sanitarium, was unable to recognize him and his father had developed a drinking problem. The honeymoon was further ruined when Grant took ill and was forced to extend his stay.

Above: Grant with Cherrill at the Desert Inn in Palm Springs, California, in November 1933. Cherrill's career had already peaked in the 1920s as Charlie Chaplin's leading lady in *City Lights*, but Grant's was taking off with the rousing success of *She Done Him Wrong*, released in January of that year. The movie saved Paramount from bankruptcy and made Cary Grant a star.

Opposite: Grant made this balancing act look easy, but he had more trouble balancing marriage and career. He was certainly working hard: he'd made fourteen films in his first three years at Paramount, which didn't leave him much time to work at his marriage. Less than a year after their wedding, Virginia Cherrill and Cary Grant filed for divorce. Cherrill cited mental cruelty as the reason she left Grant, which kept Grant's alleged jealous rages out of the papers.

Above: Cary Grant and Myrna Loy in *Wings in the Dark* (1935). Grant played a pilot blinded in a gas explosion who goes on to invent a device for navigating in fog. Loy played a female pilot whose character was modeled after Amelia Earhart. Earhart actually visited the set during the filming.

Above: After Virginia Cherrill moved out, Randolph Scott moved back in with Grant. Scott shared Grant's interest in boxing and the two were often seen at fights, escorted by whatever starlets were available. Boxing was one of the salt-of-the-earth pastimes that kept "Archie Leach" in touch with his working-class roots. He also loved baseball and cheered for the Dodgers and the Yankees.

Left: Cary Grant with Toby Wing, Mitchell Leisen, and Caesar Romero at a Hollywood party. Despite his unhappy personal life, Grant was still expected to keep up a star's social calendar in order to make the public believe what they saw on the screen.

ight: Katharine Hepburn as Sylvia/Sylvester and Cary Grant as Jimmy Monkley in *Sylvia Scarlett*, the story of an embezzler whose daughter disguises herself as a boy to avoid detection. The film has developed a cult reputation because of the ambiguous sexuality of the leads. At one point, Grant takes off his shirt, grabs "Sylvester" and says, "You'll make a proper little hot water bottle." When it was released in 1935, *Sylvia Scarlett* was a critical and commercial disaster. The studio was furious with director George Cukor for the indulgent nature of the film, but Grant got some of his first good reviews since *She Done Him Wrong*.

elow: In 1935, Grant was loaned out to RKO to make *Sylvia Scarlett*. The movie introduced Grant to Cukor, whom he credited as being the first director to get him to really open up on camera. The dark, mysterious, brooding quality of Grant's character added an important dimension to the Grant persona.

ight: Cary Grant, having just returned from his father's funeral in Bristol, England, studies his lines for *Suzy*. Grant had recently worked on *Amazing Adventure* (1936) in England in order to be near his dying father. At the funeral, he eulogized his father as "his first hero" and seemed prepared to downplay his troubled childhood in order to mourn.

elow: In 1935, Grant was loaned out to MGM to star in *Suzy* (1936) with Jean Harlow and Franchot Tone. Grant played a hotshot World War I pilot who falls in love with Suzy, played by Harlow. Although the script was reworked by several writers, including Dorothy Parker, the character Grant played was glamorous but stupid. After Andre (Grant) and Suzy marry, he goes right back to courting showgirls, and Suzy's first husband, Terry, played by Tone, returns to rescue her.

Above: Cary Grant and Jean Harlow in *Suzy*. For the first time since his singing entrance in *This Is the Night*, Grant got to show off his baritone voice. His song from *Suzy*, "Did I Remember?" was released to some success. But audiences and critics were not convinced that *Suzy* was a movie worthy of the talent of its leads. Grant glumly went back to Paramount, but he'd already decided to leave after he finished his next picture, *Wedding Present* (1936). His contract was about to expire and he didn't attempt to renew it.

Chapter Two

Screwball Guru

Opposite: Cary Grant and Irene Dunne as Jerry and Lucy Warriner in *The Awful Truth* (1937). The Warriners are a wealthy couple who suspect each other of adultery and decide to divorce. *The Awful Truth* is a smooth combination of slapstick and drawing-room comedy. The first half of the film showcases some of Grant's finest physical comedy. The plot builds to the climactic Jerry the Nipper scene, in which Lucy accuses Jerry, in front of his new fiancée and future in-laws, of being a secret drinker. Grant's under-the-breath commentary and facial expressions steal the scene. These subtle antics became his trademark, and the scene marks the moment when Cary Grant perfected his complicated onscreen persona.

Above: Hoagy Carmichael plays piano for George (Cary Grant) and Marion (Constance Bennett) Kerby in a nightclub scene from *Topper* (1937). In 1936, Cary Grant had finally completed his obligations to Paramount and became a free agent. He was the first star to willingly leave the studio system and paved the way for other independents to make it in Hollywood. This MGM supernatural screwball comedy was a hit, and the image of Cary Grant in evening wear was permanently burned into the American psyche. Grant finally had his pick of roles and top billing.

Above: "Resting's the sorta thing you've gotta work up to gradu-
ally. It's very dangerous to rest all of a sudden," says George
Kerby in *Topper*. He and his wife, Marion, manage to catch a few
winks in their car before meeting with their bank manager, the ter-
minally henpecked Cosmo Topper. *Topper* called upon one of the
most important plot devices in screwball comedy—complicated
sleeping arrangements. According to the Hays Production Code
that was instituted in the early 1930s, you couldn't show husbands
and wives sleeping in the same bed together, so writers went out
of their way to provide some outrageously entertaining alterna-
tives. "You can't sleep here," became one of the most often re-
peated lines in the genre.

Above: George and Marion Kerby after a long day teaching Cosmo Topper (Roland Young) about drinking, dancing, and dames. The Kerbys are everything that people in the movies should be: rich, carefree, fun-loving, and beautiful. They are also dreadful drivers and are killed in a car accident early in the film. As translucent shades, the ghostly glitterati need to do a good deed to get to heaven, so they set out to teach Topper how to have fun before it's too late. *Topper*, like other screwball comedies, reinforced the idea that wacky high jinks were a neccessity in life.

Left: Director Leo McCarey, Ginger Rogers, and Cary Grant on the set of *Once Upon a Honeymoon* (1942), McCarey's attempt to update screwball comedy and rekindle the magic Grant had brought to the screen in *The Awful Truth*.

Above: Irene Dunne and Cary Grant with Skippy, who is the subject of their custody battle in *The Awful Truth*. Thanks to his role as Asta in the *Thin Man* movies, Skippy was almost as big a star as Dunne and Grant. McCarey brought in confusion specialist Skippy to play the Warriners' dog, Mr. Smith, whose tricks often had disastrous consequences.

Above: Irene Dunne and Cary Grant in the moonlight at the end of *The Awful Truth*. McCarey used a virtually scriptless improvisational style to give *The Awful Truth* a spontaneous, energetic feel. Ralph Bellamy later said that McCarey would show up on the set with the day's lines and stage directions scribbled on brown paper and start the camera rolling. This deeply worried Grant, and he approached Columbia Pictures' head, Harry Cohen, about buying his way out of the film, but Cohen made him stick to it.

Left: A lobby card for *Bringing Up Baby* (1938). Director Howard Hawks had a difficult time casting the role of David Huxley. Grant refused at first, but Hawks convinced him to play the part as if he were silent-film comedian Harold Lloyd. Intrigued by the challenge, Grant signed up. Hawks' use of improvisational style as well as his obsessive attention to the details of physical comedy made *Bringing Up Baby* one of the longest, most demanding shoots of Grant's career. It went $300,000 over budget and took nearly twice as long to film as Hawks had originally planned.

Below: In this scene, David Huxley is festooned with swan feathers, all that remains of Baby's afternoon snack. Clutched tightly under his arm, he holds his "rare and precious bone," the intercostal clavicle, that George the dog (played by Skippy) will soon steal and bury in the yard.

Above: David Huxley and Susan Vance (Katharine Hepburn) on a leopard hunt in the wilds of Connecticut in *Bringing Up Baby*. For the madcap heiress, there's no ruse too complicated when it comes to catching her man. She can be flighty and scatterbrained when it suits her purposes, but the rest of the time, she outsmarts David. When David's temper flares, she blithely replies, "The love impulse in males frequently exhibits itself in terms of conflict"—a bit of pop psychology that could sum up the entire screwball genre.

Left: After Susan stole his clothes, David got saddled with an ill-fitting riding outfit. Grant's job throughout most of the film was to play straight man to Hepburn. Grant felt particularly comfortable with this role, since he'd studied George Burns and Gracie Allen from the wings as a teenager and had played the straight man in several vaudeville duos.

Above: Grant, Hepburn, May Robson as Aunt Elizabeth, Leona Roberts as Mrs. Gogarty, and Skippy as George the dog. After his famous ad-lib, "I just went gay all of a sudden," David slumps down on the stairs in frustration wearing Susan's negligee. It is one of the outrageous moments in the film where Grant breaks out of his "straight man" role. The fact that Grant was the first to use the word gay to mean homosexual in mainstream media didn't help quell the rumors that he was gay. Pauline Kael, in her essay "The Man from Dream City," said, "He is never so butch—so beefy and clumsy a he-man—as in female impersonations."

Above: Doris Nolan as Julia Seton, Katharine Hepburn as Linda Seton, Cary Grant as Johnny Case, and Edward Ayers as Ned Seton in *Holiday* (1938). This film was more low-key than Grant's other screwball comedies, but still touted the mantra of fun in its own quiet way. Johnny Case is a hardworking everyman who gets engaged to the wealthy Julia Seton. He plans to take Julia on a trip around the world so they can "find themselves," but Julia has big plans for Johnny in the family-owned bank. Hepburn plays the black-sheep sister who falls for Johnny when she isn't too busy baby-sitting her alcoholic younger brother, Ned.

Below: *Holiday* gave Grant an excellent opportunity to show off his vaudevillian tumbling skills. His character uses somersaults and other forms of play to recharge his spirit—and he takes the time to teach unconventional Linda a few tricks. When acrobatics become a screwball courtship ritual, fussy Julia doesn't stand a chance.

Chapter Three

Mid-Life Cary

Opposite: A haggard-looking Cary Grant in the late 1930s. In a short period of time, Grant had dealt with his father's death and his first divorce. He also did some of his best work, throwing himself into his independent film career, sometimes making as many as three pictures a year. While this was only half the output of his early Paramount years, the roles he took in the late thirties were a lot more demanding. The mad pace of a screwball comedy took its toll on the performers as well as the audience. Grant said after he retired that he didn't remember making the movies for which he was most famous.

Above: Victor McLaglen as MacChesney, Cary Grant as Archibald Cutter, and Edward Ciannelli as the Thuggee guru in *Gunga Din* (1939). MacChesney admonishes Cutter for attempting to loot a local temple, until he gets a proper look at his back. The screenplay added considerable comedy to Kipling's poem, such as the Monty Pythonesque scene in which Archibald is discovered in the temple. He puts on his his best English bobby impersonation and attempts to single-handedly arrest fifty or sixty men.

Above: Cary Grant, Victor McLaglen, and Douglas Fairbanks in *Gunga Din*. The producers originally wanted Howard Hawks to direct the film, but he went so over schedule and over budget on *Bringing Up Baby* that they were afraid to give him the expensive blockbuster. RKO hired instead George Stevens, who turned the film into a masterpiece of black-and-white cinematography. *Gunga Din* was also the most commercially successful movie RKO ever made.

Right: Eight shot glasses on the table and a softhearted dame to sing the blues was the Hawksian vision of a pilot's funeral. In *Only Angels Have Wings* (1939), Grant played Geoff Carter, the owner of an airborne mail-delivery service in South America. Bonnie Lee (Jean Arthur) arrives on a banana boat just before one of the pilots is killed in a landing accident. Carter's reaction is reserved—almost flippant—and his darkly comic remarks introduce the hard-nosed world of the movie.

TOGETHER FOR THE FIRST TIME

CARY GRANT ★ JEAN ARTHUR

ONLY ANGELS HAVE WINGS

THOMAS **MITCHELL** ★ RITA **HAYWORTH** ★ RICHARD **BARTHELMESS**

A HOWARD HAWKS PRODUCTION Screen play by JULES FURTHMAN **A COLUMBIA PICTURE**

A bove: Hawks redeemed his reputation as a bankable director with *Only Angels Have Wings*. He pitted spunky Jean Arthur against his young discovery, Rita Hayworth, in a love triangle with Cary Grant. But the heart of the movie was the male bonding between the pilots. The film is an action-adventure buddy picture with a little singing and dancing—and some kissing thrown in for good measure.

Opposite: Cary Grant and Carole Lombard play forbidden lovers Alec Walker and Julie Eden in *In Name Only* (1939). The stars' screwball reputations fooled everyone into thinking the film would be a divorce comedy along the lines of *The Awful Truth*, but audiences were in for a surprise. The film starts out that way, with the two meeting for a lighthearted, platonic jaunt in the woods. When their inevitable attraction surfaces, Walker is forced to reveal that he is trapped in a loveless marriage with his wealthy wife, and suddenly, the stars of *Bringing Up Baby* and *My Man Godfrey* are pulling off a melodrama. Walker must choose between money and the love of his life.

Above: Julie (Lombard) and Suzanne (Helen Vinson) rush to Alec's aid after he is thrown from the car in an accident. This was the just the first of many brushes with death he would have to endure before freeing himself of his in-name-only wife. According to the Hays Code, adulterers needed to suffer for their sins, so the couple's unconsummated passion nearly kills him before his wife is revealed to be a gold digger and he is finally able to divorce her. Both Grant's and Lombard's performances were well received by critics.

Above: Ralph Bellamy looks doubtful as Hildy's new fiancé, Bruce Baldwin, in *His Girl Friday* (1940). Conniving newspaper editor Walter Burns (Grant) uses every possible duplicity to foil his ex-wife Hildy's (played by Rosalind Russell) engagement. In this scene, he steals Baldwin's wallet and arranges to delay his train. In real life, Cary Grant introduced Rosalind Russell to her husband, Freddie Brissum. "Walter, you're wonderful in a loathsome sort of way," says Hildy. Walter Burns was a slippery character who paved the way for Grant's work with Alfred Hitchcock.

Left: (left to right) Porter Hall as Murphy, Cary Grant as Walter Burns, Gene Lockhart as Peter "B for Brains" Hartwell, and Pat West as the Warden in the frenetic conclusion of *His Girl Friday*. Hawks used ad-libbing to get spontaneous reactions and encouraged the cast to speak as quickly as possible. Many of the jokes simply flew past the censors in what was probably the fastest dialogue in cinema history, much of which was made up by Russell and Grant. In this scene, Burns snaps at the sheriff, "The last man who said that to me was Archie Leach, just before he slit his own throat."

Above: Cary Grant and Irene Dunne in *My Favorite Wife* (1940). The leopard-print robe in this scene was an inside reference to *Bringing Up Baby*. In *My Favorite Wife*, Dunne plays Ellen Arden, a woman who returns after being presumed dead for seven years to find that her husband, Nick, has just wed a shrewish bride. Leo McCarey was initially enlisted to direct the film, due to its great similarity to *The Awful Truth*, but he was injured in a car accident and Carson Ganin took over the production. *My Favorite Wife* lacked the originality and sparkle of *The Awful Truth*, but it certainly had its moments. Here, Nick confronts his first wife about her conduct during her disappearance (she lived with another man, a buff swimmer played by none other than Randolph Scott) while his new bride, wearing a matching leopard-print robe, is impatiently awaiting her wedding night in the next room.

Above: A publicity photo from *My Favorite Wife* featuring Grant and Dunne. The picture hints at the chemistry between the two stars, which best came through in their fight scenes. Dunne had developed a subtle, scene-stealing style of her own and their arguments were loaded with cooing, underhanded barbs that were almost musical.

Above: Cary Grant, Randolph Scott, and friends in the Hollywood Brown Derby, circa 1939. Grant and Scott worked together on two pictures, *Hot Saturday* and *My Favorite Wife*. The pair caused a minor scandal when they shared a hotel room at the Pacific Hotel during the filming of *My Favorite Wife*.

Left: Like *The Awful Truth*, the ending of *My Favorite Wife* features complicated sleeping arrangements. Nick, who's just received an annulment from his second wife, hasn't decided to forgive his first wife for her actions during her disappearance and is forced to haul his mattress to the attic to rethink his situation.

Below: The chemistry between Cary Grant and Jimmy Stewart was wonderful in *The Philadelphia Story*, their only film together. Stewart's Mike Connors is a more cynical, worldly version of his Mr. Smith. He brilliantly partially ad-libbed a drunken parody of a Mr. Smith–type speech in this scene with C.K. Dexter Haven (Grant), a yacht designer and recovering alcoholic. The down-on-his-luck play-boy role wasn't much of a stretch for Grant, but he gave the part depth and added sobriety to the generally madcap proceedings. Cukor managed to balance Stewart and Grant, never forcing them to compete head-to-head. Stewart got most of the good lines—and won the Oscar—while Grant occasionally stole scenes.

Above: Jimmy Stewart, Cary Grant, and Katharine Hepburn in the grand finale of *The Philadelphia Story*. The movie contains a rather pointed criticism of tabloid journalism, and in this scene, Mike Connors and Liz Imbrie (pictured just behind Stewart) give up the tabloid business to play best man and maid of honor at Tracy's and Dexter's wedding. No sooner have they put their cameras and notebooks away when another paparazzi arrives to snap this picture.

Right: As Tracy Lord, Hepburn's cool detachment toward Grant's character, C.K. Dexter Haven, is evident in this publicity photo. Her then-beau, Howard Hughes, had bought the film rights to *The Philadelphia Story* for Hepburn as a gift. Hepburn turned around and sold the rights to MGM, demanded that it be directed by George Cukor, and asked that Clark Gable and Spencer Tracy play opposite her. She got Cukor but had to "settle" for Cary Grant and Jimmy Stewart.

Above: Barbara Hutton, Cary Grant, and Rosalind Russell out on the town, circa 1940. While filming *The Philadelphia Story*, Grant was secretly romancing real-life heiress Barbara Hutton, who had inherited the Woolworth fortune and had divorced a German count when she met Grant. The couple kept their relationship a secret for fear of publicity. When they did meet in public, they added decoy Rosalind Russell for safe measure. Eventually Hutton and Grant became engaged. The headlines read "Cash and Cary." Hutton said years later that Grant was the only one of her husbands who never took a dime from her.

Above: Irene Dunne and Cary Grant teamed up with director George Stevens for the tearjerker *Penny Serenade* (1941). Grant and Dunne were both nominated for Oscars for their work in this quiet, issue-driven film about a couple unable to have children who struggle to keep their marriage alive during the adoption process.

Below: Cary Grant and Ginger Rogers in *Once Upon a Honeymoon* (1942). Grant plays Pat O'Toole, a journalist who falls in love with Katie O'Hara (Rogers), an American married to a Nazi. He helps her escape across Europe in a bizarre mixture of screwball comedy and World War II spy drama. The film was part of the Hollywood propaganda campaign to get America behind the war effort. After unsuccessfully trying to enlist in the army, Grant was informed that he would be of better service in Hollywood. Grant spied on Hitler's favorite director, Leni Reifenstahl, when she came to Hollywood to visit Walt Disney. He also used his show-business connections to keep tabs on Hollywood anti-Semites and Nazi sympathizers.

Opposite: Joan Fontaine and Cary Grant in Alfred Hitchcock's *Suspicion* (1941). Grant accepted the role of John Aynsgar on the condition that the part be softened from that of a murderer to one who only appears to be a murderer. The ambiguous nature of Aynsgar presented a unique challenge to Grant. He was required to appear both guilty and innocent at all times. The air of mystery he'd brought to earlier roles served him well in *Suspicion*. He was both playful and menacing, often within the same scene, and made these mood shifts so smoothly that no one really noticed he was doing some of his best work. Based on the novel *Before the Fact*, the film's name was changed to *Suspicion* so that the audience wouldn't know whether or not Grant's character was a killer until the last scene. Hitchcock wrote and filmed two separate endings to the film, hoping to do it his way with Aynsgar as the killer and his wife the willing victim. But early preview audiences preferred the soft ending, in which Joan Fontaine's character is so paranoid that she only imagines her husband is trying to kill her.

Above: Cary Grant and canine friend. Cary appeared dashing, square-shouldered, and completely at home in military uniforms, despite the fact that he never wore one in real life. Grant was born too late to be drafted into World War I and too early to make it into World War II, yet he became an icon of service in both wars on the movie screen.

Above: Was the ominously glowing glass of milk poisoned? That was what Lina Aynsgar (Fontaine) and the audience wondered in *Suspicion*. Hitchcock's first ending showed Cary Grant delivering the fatal glass of milk, which literally glowed, thanks to the light bulb Hitchcock had placed in it. As Fontaine takes her last breath, she writes a letter to her parents explaining that she still loves her husband although he has murdered her. This devastating commentary on the often-seductive nature of domestic violence could have made for Grant's greatest movie. But with the safe ending, Fontaine took home the Oscar for looking scared and Cary's performance was largely ignored.

Above: Cary Grant, Joan Blondell, and James Cagney perform a radio play for NBC Radio. Grant's film hits from the 1930s and early 1940s were very popular as radio adaptations. He made radio versions of *His Girl Friday*, *Mr. Blandings Builds His Dream House*, and *The Awful Truth*, and appeared on countless radio variety shows in the 1940s.

Left: Cary Grant as gambler Joe Adams and Lorraine Day as the beautiful war charity volunteer who wins his heart in *Mr. Lucky* (1943). Adams takes on a dead gangster's persona in order to dodge the draft. He and his lovable gang of thugs plan to bilk a war charity out of "two hundred Gs," until a letter from the gangster's mother describing Nazi atrocities helps him turn over a new leaf.

Opposite: Here's looking at you, Cary. The gangster tough guy he played in *Mr. Lucky* is suave, romantic, and relatively nonviolent, and eventually becomes a war hero. Mr. Lucky spends more time kissing his leading lady than committing crimes—a far cry from the gangsters that Jimmy Cagney and Humphrey Bogart made famous. Grant's character gets the girl and is redeemed without getting shot to pieces in the final scene of the movie.

Above: Cary Grant and John Garfield do a little morale boosting with a couple of visiting Waves on the set of *Destination Tokyo* in 1943. Cary played a submarine captain leading a crew of wacky misfits through a dangerous mission in Tokyo Harbor. *Destination Tokyo* started a submarine craze in Hollywood. Grant's stoic Captain Cassidy was emulated by John Wayne in *Operation Pacific* and was eventually parodied by Cary himself in *Operation Petticoat* (1959). *Destination Tokyo* was part of Hollywood's cooperation with the war effort and Roosevelt's massive propaganda campaign to mobilize the entire country.

ight: June Duprez as Ida, Cary Grant's glamorous working-class girlfriend with Grant in *None but the Lonely Heart*. The story is set in the East End of London. Born and raised in Bristol, Grant wasn't a native Cockney, but he was good at the accent, which he'd learned to imitate when he was in vaudeville. The film gave him the chance to use some of the East End's more colorful expressions, like "Anybody who'd do that oughta 'ave 'is bullocks spanked." The American censors, unaware of the intricacies of British slang, let the mild profanity slip through.

elow: "My, sheep's 'eart again, Ma? Are we so poor as to be eatin' the innards of pigs and cows day in and day out?" Ernie Mott (Cary Grant) teasingly asks his mother, played by Ethel Barrymore in *None but the Lonely Heart*. Although the character in Clifford Odets' play of the same name was a teenager, Grant fell in love with the role and convinced Odets to make Ernie Mott middle-aged for the film. Grant threw himself into the part and made the story of the struggle between mother and son poignantly his own. His own mum, whom he rescued from Fishponds Sanitarium in 1938, was always distant toward him, and their relationship was awkward at best. "The minute I get in the room with her I start clearing my throat," he once said jokingly, covering his regret that he and Elsie didn't have the friendly, sparring relationship that Ernie Mott had with his mother.

Above: Dan Duryea as gangster Len Tate and Cary Grant as Ernie Mott in *None but the Lonely Heart*. The film was Clifford Odets' directorial debut and the playwright managed a surprisingly artful, noirish movie. Odets used Wellesian deep focus and strange lighting to show the emotional distances between the characters. The film's plot is quite melodramatic, yet it is saved by a dark sense of humor, much of which was provided by Cary Grant's plucky portrayal of Ernie Mott.

Above: Cary Grant and Betty Hansel at the Mocambo. At the time this photograph was taken, Grant was separated from his second wife, Barbara Hutton. The press fixated on Hansel and blamed her for the divorce, but all parties involved vehemently denied that his friendship with Hansel was the source of his marital problems. Hutton said in divorce court that she and Grant were simply incompatible and had difficulty living together. She enjoyed entertaining her well-to-do friends with elaborate dinner parties, while Cary was uncomfortable with her crowd and became an outsider in his own home. Grant and Hutton were both prone to bouts with depression, and the lack of a stable caretaker in the relationship doomed it from the start.

Opposite: Cary Grant as secret agent T.R. Devlin in *Notorious* (1946). Devlin was Cary's darkest character, a man who let his jealous insecurity interfere with his professional responsibilities, nearly allowing Alicia Huberman, played by Ingrid Bergman, to be killed in the line of duty. Hitchcock built an almost unbearable suspense around the love story between two government operatives, one of whom is forced sleep with a Nazi. Like Walter Burns in *His Girl Friday*, Devlin tries to use the confused situation to manipulate a commitment from Bergman without offering one of his own. But the plan backfires when Alicia, whose self-esteem is crushed by Devlin's manipulation, agrees to marry the Nazi, who is at least unabashedly in love with her.

Above: Cary enjoyed working with Hitch. He and costar Ingrid Bergman posed as the "Master of Suspense" pretended to push them on a cart during the filming of *Notorious*. Hitchcock was one of the few directors in whom Grant had confidence. The result was a seemingly effortless performance as a James Bond prototype with a tortured inner life. Grant also got along famously with Bergman, and they formed a long-standing friendship.

Opposite: "I was a fat-headed guy full of pain," Dev confesses to Alicia during their famous one-shot embrace that is the unforgettable climax of *Notorious*. Dev's vulnerability isn't really revealed until this scene. *Notorious* is an example of how Grant managed to portray complex, multilevel characters in what were essentially Hollywood genre pictures.

Chapter Four

The Beau Ideal

Opposite: Grant's attempts at conventionally dramatic roles in *None but the Lonely Heart* and *Penny Serenade* offered him little satisfaction, and he considered retiring from movies altogether. Ultimately, though, his work proved to be the one stable element in his life, and he continued to make pictures in which his persona was taken for granted from the first frame. He became the ultimate catch, and his onscreen pursuers were well aware of his status as the world's most desirable bachelor. This "Beau Ideal," to borrow a phrase from film historian Gael McSweeney, had polished looks and urbane manners to match and was presented by Hollywood as the ideal to which every man should aspire. Often, the dignified Beau Ideal was a comic foil, sent into awkward, humorous situations while his female lead waited for him to topple from his pedestal and into her waiting arms.

Above: Cary Grant is strapped into his suit of shining armor for *The Bachelor and the Bobby-Soxer* (1947). With a script that was one of romance novelist Sydney Sheldon's early creations, it was the story of a teenager's crush on Dick Nugent (Grant), a dashing middle-aged gentleman. Fun-loving Myrna Loy of the *Thin Man* series plays Margaret, the older sister of teen-age Susan (a grown-up Shirley Temple). Margaret compels Nugent to spend time with Susan in order to cure the lovelorn teenager of her crush. After struggling to make serious, difficult pictures, Cary Grant effortlessly strolled through *The Bachelor and the Bobby-Soxer*, which became a big hit.

Above: Grant, Temple, and Johnny Sands in *The Bachelor and the Bobby-Soxer*. The movie was saved from being too cute by Nugent's reactions to Susan's advances. Grant was used to being pursued by females onscreen, but none this young. The setup provided plenty of opportunities for Grant's quiet scene-stealing as he mocked the oh-so-serious teens.

Above: Jerry White (Rudy Vallee) and Dick Nugent (Grant) vie for Margaret's affection in *The Bachelor and the Bobby-Soxer*. Believing that the victor in this silly contest would win Margaret's heart, Jerry challenges Dick to a potato-balancing race. Dick hopes his newly found "teen spirit" will discourage Susan, whose interest in him is based on the fact that he is a sophisticated older man.

Right: Cary Grant as harp-playing heavenly visitor Dudley in the holiday favorite *The Bishop's Wife* (1947). From a knight in shining armor to an earthbound angel, Grant became a celestial Beau Ideal in this film. He was originally cast as the bishop and David Niven had the role of the angel, but after reading the script, Grant decided Dudley the angel was the better part and used his star power to get recast. Grant was intrigued by the idea of an angel sent to fix a bishop's marriage but who ends up falling in love himself. *The Bishop's Wife* afforded Grant a rare opportunity to play a character who feels unrequited love.

Opposite: Cary Grant and his soon-to-be third wife, Betsy Drake, at the 1947 Oscars. Grant first spotted Drake in a play in London and then bumped into her on the ship back to America. The young actress was headed to Hollywood for a screen test, and Grant offered to help her into the business. She got her first role, starring opposite him, in *Every Girl Should Be Married* (1948).

Above: Dore Scharey directs Myrna Loy, Melvyn Douglas, and Cary Grant in *Mr. Blandings Builds His Dream House* (1948). While Grant settled down in the big-screen suburbs, America's taste in movies was changing, and although he was still a popular leading man for romantic comedies, this was the era of raw, sexual leading men like Marlon Brando, James Dean, and Montgomery Clift.

Below: Cary Grant and Myrna Loy on the set of *Mr. Blandings Builds His Dream House*. As the dignified Mrs. Blandings, Loy relied on her cool wit to play straight man to Grant's manic character. Her part was heroic but underwritten, and it was a shame that she and Grant were never put into a no-holds-barred screwball scene together. However, there was some good verbal sparring in the film, which echoed the actors' screwball pasts. "I don't know why I married you," says a frustrated Mrs. Blandings. "Maybe it was that ridiculous hole in your chin!"

Above: The Blandingses and their daughters, Joan (left, played by Sharyn Moffett) and Betsy (right, played by Connie Marshall). The film was remarkably popular with the millions of people moving to the suburbs who could relate to the sufferings of Jim Blandings. Of course, most of them didn't have live-in maids like Mrs. Blandings did. The Blandingses were an early version of the television sitcom family that would become popular in shows like *Father Knows Best* and *Leave It to Beaver*. It was particularly fitting that Jim Blandings was an advertising man, a profession that figured heavily in the postwar economy. In a sense, Grant was also an ad-man, selling his image of the ideal modern family who eventually adjust to their surburban environment and live happily ever after in their new home.

Below: Lieut. Catherine Gates (Ann Sheridan) smuggles Henri Rochard (Cary Grant) in drag onto a naval destroyer in *I Was a Male War Bride* (1949). Rochard is a GI who, upon release from the army, finds the girl of his dreams. Unfortunately, she's still enlisted. The movie was Howard Hawks' attempt to update the screwball comedy of the 1930s to fit current events. During production, Grant developed jaundice and nearly died. His illness was fodder for Howard Hawks' black humor. The beginning of the film was shot at a Hollywood studio after Grant had recovered; Hawks inserted a joke about jaundice into the scene.

Above: Cary Grant and Jeanne Crain in *People Will Talk* (1951). Grant plays Noah Pretorious, a popular obstetrician who marries his suicidal patient. The plot is part melodrama, part love story, and part meditation on the death penalty. Somehow it all works with comic relief provided by Dr. Pretorious. Joseph Mancewicz directed and adapted the screenplay for *People Will Talk*, and his trademark moralizations did not help the film with audiences. The threads of Mancewicz's script were too far-flung to live up to his Oscar-winning *All About Eve*, and Grant completed yet another competent seriocomic portrayal that was quickly forgotten.

eft: Betsy Drake and Cary Grant in their second film together, *Room for One More* (1952). After the movie's mediocre box-office results, the couple decided to take an extended break from Hollywood and devoted themselves to traveling to exotic locations and to the study of languages and musical instruments. But Cary was still deeply troubled and depressed. Drake introduced him to therapy, and it was under her doctor's care that he had intensive hypnosis treatments that used LSD to elicit the actor's repressed memories of his early childhood. Grant always credited Betsy with helping him resolve his troubled past and the long-buried feelings of abandonment that stemmed from the disappearance of his mother.

elow: Howard Hawks directs Cary Grant with Hawks' newest discovery, Marilyn Monroe, in *Monkey Business* (1952). Unlike the rest of America, Grant was not enchanted by Marilyn. His vaudevillian work ethic made her lack of professionalism appalling to him.

Above: Robert Cornthwaite, Cary Grant, and Bubbles the chimp in *Monkey Business*. Grant plays a scientist who invents a fountain-of-youth formula, which he and his wife, played by Ginger Rogers, take by accident. The gimmick-filled plot was considered beneath both the star and the director in 1952. "It was the period of blue jeans, dope addicts and Method [acting] and nobody cared about comedy at all," Cary said, eloquently summing up the change that came over Hollywood in the 1950s.

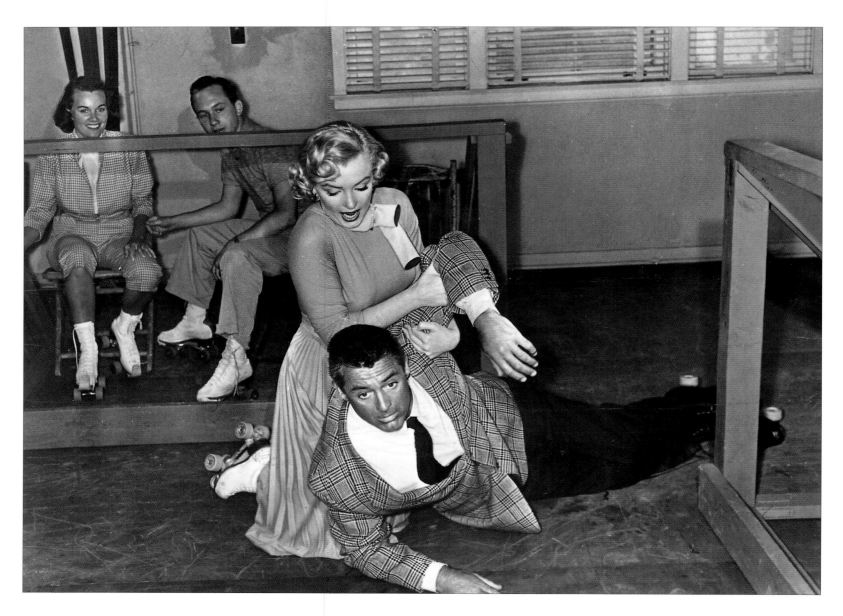

Above: Cary Grant and Marilyn Monroe in *Monkey Business*. In an odd way, Hawks managed to change the shape of Grant's career a fourth time with this film. He made Cary Grant, the Beau Ideal, a bit of a nerd. Grant's character, Barnaby Fulton, goes, pardon the pun, bananas, when he takes the youth formula and gets a hideous crew cut, a tacky plaid sport coat, a convertible, and a painfully awkward date with Marilyn Monroe.

Opposite: Grant tests out his costume for *Dream Wife* (1953). In the film he plays Clemson Reade, an American who breaks off a relationship with career woman, Priscilla Effington (Deborah Kerr), to get engaged to a princess from the fictional country of Bukistan. After veering off course in *Monkey Business*, Grant was back to his old suave self in his first film with Deborah Kerr. Grant and Kerr made three more movies together after *Dream Wife*, and their onscreen romantic pairing became one of the most memorable of Grant's career.

WARDROBE STILL
PROD NO. 1607 DATE 9-20-52
ACTOR CARY GRANT
CHARACTER CLEM
CHANGE # 19 DESIGNER
SCENE 93
COLOR B&W X COSTUMER ARRIGO

Below: Cary Grant as John Robie the Cat in Alfred Hitchcock's *To Catch a Thief* (1955). Along with his dark, handsome looks, Cary's superb balance and lithe grace were qualities that were unaffected by his age. The skills he had learned as a stilt walker in the Pender Troupe were important in the rooftop scenes of this film. Grant had to overcome an aversion to heights for the part. Grant was sleek but provincial when necessary—in the midst of the movie's catfight between Grace Kelly and French femme fatale Brigitte Auber.

Above: Sophia Loren and Cary Grant in *The Pride and the Passion*. Grant took a great liking to his costar. Their whirlwind romance ended with Grant (who was still married to Betsy Drake at the time) proposing marriage to Loren. Grant found out later, after Loren had accepted Betsy's role in *Houseboat* (1958), that she had been secretly engaged to Carlo Ponti the whole time.

Opposite: *The Pride and the Passion* (1957) was one Cary Grant movie where the events on the set were far more exciting than they were on the screen. Frank Sinatra, pictured here, left the set before filming was complete. Perhaps he noticed Cary smirking at his bad Spanish accent.

Below: Cary Grant and Betsy Drake, circa 1957. While Grant was romancing Loren on the set of *The Pride and the Passion*, Betsy was nearly drowned in a ferry accident in which fifty other passengers died. Somewhat red-faced after his debacle with Loren, Grant rushed off to comfort Betsy and salvage his marriage.

Above: Completely on the other end of the spectrum from his suave and sophisticated onscreen persona, Grant posed for this less-than-dignified publicity photo during the filming of *The Pride and the Passion* in Spain.

Above: Cary Grant during the filming of *Indiscreet* (1958).
Including *Indiscreet*, Grant made four fairly unremarkable movies
with director Stanley Donen. Donen and Grant formed an independent production company, and Cary was the first Hollywood
star to produce his own films. *Indiscreet* also showcased Ingrid
Bergman's comedic talents and was successful at the box office.
Donen and Grant proved that you didn't need great scripts or orig-
inal ideas to make hit movies. Grant knew what audiences expected
of him, and he delivered it cheerfully. "The best thing about acting in
movies is there's no heavy lifting," Grant once quipped, and with
Stanley Donen at the helm, there wasn't a lot of stretching, either.

Right: Cary Grant as Roger Thornhill and Eva Marie Saint as Eve Kendall in *North by Northwest*. "What do you do when you're not luring men to their doom on the Twentieth Century Limited?" Roger asks Eve. Just then the train lurches and she tumbles into his arms. This wasn't the first time that public transport worked to his romantic advantage. There was a cooperative cable car in *Kiss Them for Me* (1957) and a claustrophobic submarine in *Operation Petticoat*, and in real life, Cary Grant met Betsy Drake when the ship they were on tilted and she fell into him.

Below: Grant in *North by Northwest* (1959). In Alfred Hitchcock's action-packed thriller, even a scene at an art auction ends in a fistfight. Grant plays Roger Thornhill, an advertising executive who unwittingly gets drawn into a web of international intrigue. Hitch put Cary through some rigorous paces. It's fascinating to watch Thornhill slowly adapt to his new life as a spy. In this scene, Thornhill starts a fight to get himself arrested so that the "bad guys" won't kill him.

Above: Eve Kendall (Saint) shoots Thornhill (Grant) in *North by Northwest*. The intricate plot called for Grant to do some fairly rigorous stunts, like this serious pratfall. *North by Northwest* was the closest Hitchcock ever got to screwball comedy.

Opposite: Cary Grant in perhaps the most famous photograph ever taken of him, from *North by Northwest*. The crop-dusting scene is the one that most people think of when they recall the movie. A "plane dustin' crops where ain't no crops" is the source of one of Hitchcock's most terrifying sequences. Setting the scene in a wide-open plain in broad daylight, Hitchcock probed the same feelings of isolation inspired by the Midwestern landscape that would later inform the Coen brothers' 1996 thriller *Fargo*.

Above: Thornhill and Eve scramble down Mount Rushmore in *North by Northwest*. Taking advantage of the exotic South Dakota location, Hitchcock set the movie's climax on the famous national monument. Thornhill saves Eve from the bad guys and a life of spinsterhood when he proposes marriage in the shadow of Teddy Roosevelt's nose.

Opposite: Cary Grant with Kim Novak at Cannes in May 1959. Grant was enormously skillful at channeling his movie persona into real life, especially when there was a camera around. Grant was still married to Betsy Drake; this public dance with Novak kept his name in the papers the whole summer.

Above: Cary Grant and Joan O'Brien in *Operation Petticoat* (1959). Cary plays submarine commander Matt Sherman, who has little tolerance for the wackiness of his crew. Despite a number of obvious similarities to *Destination Tokyo*, *Operation Petticoat* was Grant's biggest hit to date. Audiences adored watching stiff Matt Sherman trying to keep his cool in embarrassingly close quarters with the opposite sex.

Opposite: Cary Grant admires Doris Day's shoulders in a scene from *That Touch of Mink* (1962). The plot revolves around America's favorite goody-two-shoes playing Kathy Timberlake, a woman who is undecided about whether to live in sin with a man nicknamed "Rasputin" (Grant). Doris Day's naive, Midwestern Kathy is a precursor to Marlo Thomas' "That Girl." She is so panicked at the thought of spending a night alone with Rasputin that she developes a rash just thinking about it. Eventually Rasputin changes his bachelor ways and agrees to marry her.

Above: Cary Grant as Walter Eckland in *Father Goose* (1964). Grant plays a retired school teacher who has just conned himself a very nice little yacht when he gets impressed into becoming a shoreline plane spotter for the U.S. Navy. Grant is perfectly charming as the drunken, disheveled, unpatriotic, foul-mouthed antithesis of his own persona. Grant said after his retirement that *Father Goose* was his favorite movie because he didn't have to shave during the production.

Right: Walter Eckland (Grant) is bitten by one of the girls in *Father Goose*. In the film, Eckland rescues a boat full of schoolgirls and their teacher, Catharine Freneaú, played by Leslie Caron, and they are all stranded on a less-than-Edenlike tropical island. Of course, Eckland and Catharine get down quickly to the business of playing Adam and Eve while the girls steal the show.

Above: Sidney Poitier visits with director Ralph Nelson, Leslie Caron, and Cary Grant on the set of *Father Goose*. Warren Beatty, who was courting Caron at the time, was also a frequent guest on the set.

Opposite: Cary Grant in his boxers at the Olympics in his final movie, *Walk Don't Run* (1966). Grant plays Sir William Rutland, a businessman who, during a Tokyo housing shortage, takes a room with a young English woman and an American Olympic walker. Rutland sets out to bring the two young people together. It is strange but touching to see him above the fray of the sort of goofy romantic entanglements that were his trademark for years. One almost expects him to rush in and steal the girl at the last minute. But in the final scene, Rutland watches the young couple from the street below their room and moves the rice paper screen over the window with a remote control. Then Grant quietly gets in a cab and rides offscreen forever. *Walk Don't Run* was a classy, elegant ending to an unforgettable career on film.

Chapter Five

After the Hollywood Years

Opposite: Cary Grant and Dyan Cannon with their daughter, Jennifer, in 1966. Grant's marriage to Cannon lasted less than two years but it produced his only child; he was sixty-three at the time.

Above: Newlyweds Cary Grant and Dyan Cannon arrived in Bristol in August 1965 to visit Cary's mother. Cannon was thirty-four years his junior.

Above: Paul Newman, Cary Grant, and Joanne Woodward circa 1969. The actors enjoy a beer outside Newman's trailer on the set of Newman and Woodward's movie *Winning*.

Right: Grant as he appeared in the 1970s. After retiring from the movie business, he worked first as a spokesman for Fabergé perfumes and then as a member of the company's board of directors.

Above: Cary Grant accepted his first and only Oscar in 1970, four years after he stopped making films. His former costar, Frank Sinatra, who had long since settled his differences with Grant from the filming of *The Pride and the Passion*, presented the award to Grant, who was totally overcome by the moment.

Right: Cary Grant and his fifth wife, Barbara Harris, at a New York City Friars' Roast in his honor. Grant straightened his bowtie just as the photographer snapped his picture, making it appear that he was striking a pose of girlish excitement about the roast.

Conclusion

A bove: A publicity head shot of Cary Grant from the late 1940s. Grant's face always seemed to be of a certain age: not too old, not too young, and certainly not dated. His clothes were usually simple but elegant. Pictures of Grant from this era are timeless.

O pposite: Cary Grant as he looked in the 1940s, the way his fans remember him. The former vaudevillian spent his final days on the road, visiting many of the small towns he'd played in his youth as a music-hall performer.

I n 1986, Cary Grant embarked on a speaking tour of the Midwest, which gave his fans one last chance to meet the matinee idol. Looking as spry and dashing as ever, Grant would often pull women named "Judy" out of the audience and humor them with his famous line, "Judy, Judy, Judy." Although Grant never said the line in a movie, he was always glad to repeat his trademark phrase to the delight of his fans. But the "Evenings with Cary Grant" were cut short. On November 11, 1986, Grant died suddenly of a stroke in Davenport, Iowa, at the age of eighty-two.

Grant is as popular today as ever. One of his best films, *North by Northwest*, was recently spruced up to make the rounds in revival houses around the country. There is something glamorous about going to see a Cary Grant movie on the big screen. Whether playing a nerdy paleontologist, a murderous husband, a father moving his family to the suburbs, or the disheveled captain of a yacht, Grant's timeless charm and sophistication make him appealing in any role. And that timeless quality is what touches the lives of ordinary people, young and old.

Television, the historical nemesis of the movie industry, is chiefly responsible for Grant's continuing popularity. Cable and home video have made him accessible to almost everyone. But for those who have only seen him on television, it is difficult to describe the shock of seeing a twelve-foot-tall Cary Grant stroll across the screen. This is the power of larger-than-life imagery that swept audiences away during the Great Depression when his screwball comedies were an antidote for a country's ills. It is easy to see why, over the years, audiences have gone to sit in the dark and gaze up at Cary Grant in all his urbane glory.

Filmography

Singapore Sue. Paramount (1931) (credited as
  Archie Leach).
This Is the Night. Paramount (1932).
Sinners in the Sun. Paramount (1932).
Merrily We Go to Hell. Paramount (1932).
Madame Butterfly. Paramount (1932).
Hot Saturday. Paramount (1932).
The Devil and the Deep. Paramount (1932).
Blonde Venus. Paramount (1932).
Woman Accused. Paramount (1933).
She Done Him Wrong. Paramount (1933).
I'm No Angel. Paramount (1933).
Gambling Ship. Paramount (1933).
The Eagle and the Hawk. Paramount (1933).
Alice in Wonderland. Paramount (1933).
Thirty Day Princess. Paramount (1934).
Ladies Should Listen. Paramount (1934).
Kiss and Make Up. Paramount (1934).
Born To Be Bad. United Artists/20th Century Pictures
  (1934).
Wings in the Dark. Paramount (1935).
Sylvia Scarlett. RKO (1935).
The Last Outpost. Paramount (1935).
Enter Madame. Paramount (1935).
The Wedding Present. MGM (1936).
Suzy. MGM (1936).
Big Brown Eyes. Paramount (1936).
Amazing Adventure. United Artists/Empire Films
  (1936) (a.k.a. The Amazing Quest of Ernest Bliss);
  The Amazing Quest; Riches and Romance;
  Romance and Riches.
When You're in Love. Columbia (1937).
Topper. Hal Roach Studios/MGM (1937).
The Toast of New York. RKO (1937).
The Awful Truth. Columbia (1937).
Holiday. Columbia (1938) (a.k.a. Free To Live;
  Unconventional Linda).
Bringing Up Baby. RKO (1938).
Only Angels Have Wings. Columbia (1939).
In Name Only. RKO (1939).
Gunga Din. RKO (1939).
The Philadelphia Story. MGM (1940).
My Favorite Wife. RKO (1940).
The Howards of Virginia. Columbia (1940) (a.k.a.
  The Tree of Liberty).
His Girl Friday. Columbia (1940).
Suspicion. RKO (1941).
Penny Serenade. Columbia (1941).
The Talk of the Town. Columbia (1942).
Once Upon a Honeymoon. RKO (1942).
Mr. Lucky. RKO (1943).
Destination Tokyo. Warner Bros. (1943).
Once Upon a Time. Columbia (1944).
None But the Lonely Heart. RKO (1944).
Arsenic and Old Lace. Warner Bros. (1944).
Without Reservations. RKO (1946) (cameo) (a.k.a.
  Thanks God, I'll Take It From Here) (1946).
Notorious. RKO (1946).
Night and Day. Warner Bros. (1946).
The Bishop's Wife. RKO (1947).
The Bachelor and the Bobby-Soxer. RKO (1947) (a.k.a.
  Bachelor Knight).
Mr. Blandings Builds His Dream House. RKO (1948).
Every Girl Should Be Married. RKO (1948).
I Was a Male War Bride. 20th Century Fox (1949)
  (a.k.a. You Can't Sleep Here).

Crisis. MGM (1950).
People Will Talk. 20th Century Fox (1951).
Room for One More. Warner Bros. (1952) (a.k.a. The
  Easy Way).
Monkey Business. 20th Century Fox (1952) (a.k.a.
  Darling I Am Growing Younger).
Dream Wife. MGM (1953).
To Catch a Thief. Paramount (1955).
The Pride and the Passion. United Artists (1957).
Kiss Them for Me. 20th Century Fox (1957).
An Affair to Remember. 20th Century Fox (1957).
Indiscreet. Grandon/Warner Bros. (1958).
Houseboat. Paramount (1958).
Operation Petticoat. Universal Pictures (1959).
North by Northwest. MGM (1959).
The Grass Is Greener. Grandon (1960).
That Touch of Mink. Granley Co./Universal (1962).
Charade. Universal (1963).
Father Goose. Universal (1964).
Walk Don't Run. Columbia (1966).

Bibliography

Anger, Kenneth. Hollywood Babylon II. New
  York: E.P. Dutton, Inc., 1984.

Buehrer, Beverley Bare. Cary Grant: A Bio-
  Bibliography. New York: Glenwood
  Press, 1990.

Diamandiapolis, Zoe. Cary Grant: An Internet
  Biography. 1996. Available on the
  Internet at:
  http://:www.wintermute.com/CG.html.

Donaldson, Maureen, and William Royce.
  An Affair to Remember: My Life With
  Cary Grant. New York: G.P. Putnam's
  Sons, 1989.

Higham, Charles, and Roy Moseley. Cary
  Grant: The Lonely Heart. New York:
  Harcourt, Brace, Jovanovich, 1989.

Jewell, Richard B. "How Howard Hawks
  Brought Baby Up." Journal of Popular
  Film and Television, vol 11, no. 4
  (winter 1984).

Kael, Pauline. "Cary Grant—The Man From
  Dream City," in When the Lights Go
  Down. New York: Holt, Rinehart and
  Winston, 1975.

Mast, Gerald, ed. Bringing Up Baby. New
  Brunswick, N.J.: Rutgers University
  Press, 1994.

McCann, Graham. Cary Grant: A Class Apart.
  New York: Columbia University Press,
  1997.

Schickel, Richard. Cary Grant: A Celebration.
  Boston: Little, Brown and Company,
  1983.

Sirkov, Ed. Screwball: Hollywood's Madcap
  Romantic Comedies. New York: Crown
  Publishers, Inc., 1989.

Sweeney, Gael. Falling to Earth: Reading
  British Masculinity in American Film
  Culture. Syracuse, NY: Syracuse
  University, 1997.

Wansell, Geoffrey. Haunted Idol. New York:
  William Morrow and Company, Inc., 1985.

Photography Credits

Archive Photos: pp. 10, 12, 14, 20 left, 29 top, 30
top, 34, 39, 48 bottom, 54, 63 bottom, 70 bottom,
82, 86, 89; ©Tom Gates: p. 91 bottom; ©Darlene
Hammond: p. 64; pictorial parade: p. 55 bottom;
RKO Radio: p. 31 top

Corbis-Bettmann: p. 47 top

The Kobal Collection: pp. 6, 13, 17, 19, 22 right,
31 bottom, 36, 43, 46, 49, 52 top, 60, 61, 68, 70 top,
74, 78, 79 bottom, 80 top, 80 bottom, 84, 90 top, 92

Michael Ochs Archive: pp. 73, 90 bottom, 93

Courtesy of THE MUNY: p. 11

Museum of Modern Art: pp. 2, 9, 15, 16 left, 18
top, 18 bottom, 21, 22 top left, 22 bottom left, 23
top, 23 bottom, 24 top, 24 bottom, 25, 26, 27, 28, 29
bottom, 30 bottom, 32 top, 33, 35, 37, 38 top, 38
bottom, 40, 41, 42 bottom, 44, 45 top, 45 bottom,
47 bottom, 48 top, 50 left, 50 right, 51, 52 bottom,
53, 55 top, 56 top, 56 bottom, 57, 58, 59, 62, 63 top,
65, 66-67, 67, 69, 71, 72, 76 right, 77, 79 top, 83, 85
bottom, 87

Penguin/Corbis-Bettmann: p. 81

Springer/ Corbis-Bettmann: pp. 42 top, 75

UPI/ Corbis-Bettmann: pp. 8, 16 right, 20 right,
32 bottom, 76 left, 85 top, 88, 91 top

Index

A

Academy Awards (Oscars), 46, 48, 50, 91
Alice in Wonderland (1933), 18, *18*
Allen, Gracie, 32
Amazing Adventure (1936), 24, *24*
Arlen, Richard, 18, *18*
Arthur, Jean, 38, *38, 39*
Auber, Brigitte, 74
Awful Truth, The (1937), *26,* 27, 29, 30, *30,* 43
Ayers, Edward, 34, *34*

B

Bachelor and the Bobby-Soxer, The (1947), 61, 62, *62,* 63, *63*
Bankhead, Tallulah, 14, *14*
Barrymore, Ethel, 55, *55*
Beatty, Warren, 86
Bellamy, Ralph, 30, 42, *42*
Bennett, Constance, 27, *27*
Bergman, Ingrid, 56, 58, *58, 59,* 78
Bishop's Wife, The (1947), 63, *63*
Blondell, Joan, 52, *52*
Blonde Venus (1932), 15, *15,* 18
Bogart, Humphrey, 52
Bringing Up Baby (1938), 31, *31,* 32, *32,* 38, 43
Brissum, Freddie, 42
Burns, George, 32

C

Cagney, James, 52, *52*
Cannon, Dyan, *88,* 89, *89*
Carmichael, Hoagy, 27, *27*
Caron, Leslie, 85, *85,* 86, *86*
Carroll, Nancy, 16, *16*
Celluloid Closet, The, 16
Chaplin, Charlie, 20
Cherrill, Virginia, 20, *20,* 22
Ciannelli, Edward, 37, *37*
Cohen, Harry, 30
Columbia Pictures, 30
Cooper, Gary, 14
Cornthwaite, Robert, 71, *71*
Craine, Jeanne, 69, *69*
Cukor, George, 23, 46, 47

D

Day, Doris, *84,* 85
Day, Lorraine, 52, *52*
Destination Tokyo (1943), 54, *54*
Devil and the Deep, The (1932), 14, *14*
"Did I Remember?," 25
Dietrich, Marlene, 15, *15*
Dimita, Lily, 13, *13*
Disney, Walt, 49
Donen, Stanley, 78
Douglas, Melvyn, 65, *65*
Drake, Betsy, *64,* 65, 70, *70,* 75, 76, *76,* 79, 83
Dream Wife (1953), 72
Dunne, Irene, *26,* 27, 30, *30,* 43, *43,* 44, *44,* 48, *48*
Duprez, June, 55, *55*
Duryea, Dan, 56, *56*

E

Earhart, Amelia, 22
"Evenings with Cary Grant," 93
Every Girl Should Be Married (1948), 65

F

Fairbanks, Douglas, 10, *10,* 38, *38*
Father Goose (1964), 85, *85,* 86
Fontaine, Joan, 50, *50, 51*

G

Gable, Clark, 47
Ganin, Carson, 43
Garfield, John, 54, *54*
Grant, Cary
    comedy roles, 26–35
    divorce, 20, 37, 56
    early career, 12–25
    marriages, 20, 56, 65, 76, 88, 89, 91
    radio performances, 52, *52*
    rumors about, 16, 33, 45
    straight-man roles, 32, 33
    war role, 49, 50, 54
    Grant, Jennifer, *88,* 89
    Great Depression, 11, 16
Gunga Din (1939), 37, *37,* 38, *38*

H

Hall, Porter, 42, *42*
Hansel, Betty, 56, *56*
Harlow, Jean, 24, *24,* 25, *25*
Harris, Barbara, 91, *91*
Hawks, Howard, 31, 38, 39, 42, 68, 70, *70,* 72
Hays Production Code, 28, 41
Hayworth, Rita, 39
Hepburn, Katharine, 23, *23,* 32, *32,* 33, *33,* 34, *34, 35,* 47, *47*
His Girl Friday (1940), 42, *42,* 56
Hitchcock, Alfred, 42, 50, 56, 58, *58,* 74, 79, 80
Holiday (1938), 34, *34,* 35, *35*
Hot Saturday (1939), 45, *45*
Houseboat (1958), 75
Hughes, Howard, 47
Hutton, Barbara, 48, *48,* 56, *56*

I

I'm No Angel (1933), 19, *19*
Indiscreet (1958), 78, *78*
In Name Only (1939), *40,* 41
I Was a Male War Bride (1949), 68, *68*

K

Kael, Pauline, 33
Kelly, Grace, 74
Kerr, Deborah, 72
Kiss Them for Me (1957), 79

L

Laughton, Charles, 14
Leisen, Mitchell, 22, *22*
Lloyd, Harold, 31
Lockhart, Gene, 42, *42*
Lombard, Carole, *40,* 41, *41*
Loren, Sophia, 76, 77, *77*
Loy, Myrna, 22, *22,* 61, 65, *65,* 66, *66*

M

Mancewicz, Joseph, 69
Marshall, Connie, 67, *67*